NEED A REFRESHER ON KNIT
Watch our technique videos made just for you!

Dishcloths
for Special Days

What's better for kitchen cleanup than a thirsty cotton dishcloth? A bright and happy holiday dishcloth! Representing seven fun days, these 21 designs by Julie A. Ray are quick to make using only knit and purl stitches. Choose between following written instructions or charts, and check out our free online videos for extra help. Enjoy!

LEISURE ARTS, INC. • Maumelle, Arkansas

VALENTINE'S DAY

Finished Size:
7¾"w x 9¾"h (19.5 cm x 25 cm)

The **dishcloths** can be made by following the written instructions or by following the chart for Rows 9-57 *(see Charts, page 30)*. Only **odd numbered** rows are charted. Refer to Row 8 for all **even numbered** rows.

SHOPPING LIST

Yarn (Medium Weight Cotton)
[2.5 ounces, 120 yards
(71 grams, 109 meters) per ball]:
☐ One ball for **each** Dishcloth

Knitting Needles
☐ Straight, size 8 (5 mm)
or size needed for gauge

GAUGE INFORMATION

In Stockinette Stitch
(knit one row, purl one row),
9 sts and 13 rows = 2" (5 cm)

INSTRUCTIONS
Love

Cast on 35 sts.

Rows 1-7: Knit across.

Row 8 AND ALL WRONG SIDE ROWS
THROUGH Row 58: K5, P 25, K5.

Rows 9 and 11: Knit across.

Row 13: K7, P9, K6, P3, K 10.

Row 15: K7, P9, K5, P5, K9.

Row 17: K7, (P2, K5) twice, P5, K9.

Row 19: K 14, P2, K4, P3, K1, P3, K8.

Row 21: K 11, P5, K4, P2, K3, P2, K8.

Row 23: K 11, P5, (K3, P3) twice, K7.

Row 25: K7, P2, K5, P2, K3, P2, K5, P2, K7.

Rows 27 and 29: K7, P9, K3, P2, K5, P2, K7.

Rows 31, 33, and 35: Knit across.

Row 37: K 11, P1, K7, P9, K7.

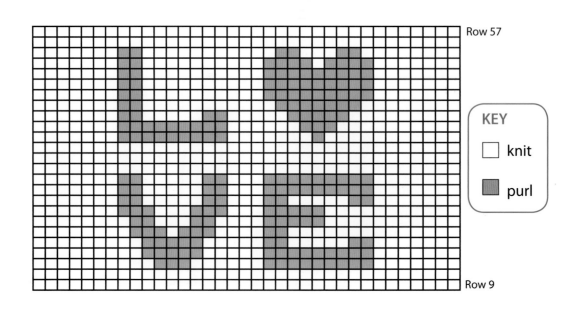

Row 57

KEY
☐ knit
▨ purl

Row 9

Love

Be Mine

Rose

Row 39: K 10, P3, K6, P9, K7.

Row 41: K9, P5, (K5, P2) twice, K7.

Row 43: K8, P7, K 11, P2, K7.

Rows 45, 47, and 49: K7, P9, K 10, P2, K7.

Row 51: K7, P4, K1, P4, K 10, P2, K7.

Row 53: K8, P2, K3, P2, K 11, P2, K7.

Rows 55 and 57: Knit across.

Rows 59-65: Knit across.

Bind off all sts in **knit**.

Rose

Cast on 35 sts.

Rows 1-7: Knit across.

Row 8 AND ALL WRONG SIDE ROWS THROUGH Row 58: K5, P 25, K5.

Row 9: Knit across.

Row 11: K 13, P4, K 18.

Row 13: K 12, P6, K2, P3, K 12.

Row 15: K 11, P7, K1, P5, K 11.

Row 17: K 10, P 16, K9.

Row 19: K9, P 18, K8.

Row 21: K9, P5, K5, P8, K8.

Row 23: K9, P4, K1, P5, K2, P6, K8.

Row 25: K8, P1, K1, P2, K1, P4, K2, P2, K1, P5, K8.

Row 27: K7, (P4, K1) twice, P5, K1, P3, K9.

Row 29: K6, P5, K1, P3, K1, P1, K2, P3, (K1, P2) twice, K7.

Row 31: K6, (P4, K1) twice, P3, K1, P2, K1, P6, K6.

Row 33: K7, P3, K1, P3, K2, P3, K1, P2, K1, P6, K6.

Row 35: K8, P2, K1, P3, K1, (P1, K1) twice, P2, K1, P1, K1, P5, K6.

Row 37: K7, (P3, K1) twice, P2, K4, P2, K1, P4, K7.

Row 39: K7, P4, K1, P2, K1, P7, K1, P4, K8.

Row 41: K7, P5, K1, P1, (K1, P6) twice, K7.

Row 43: K7, P6, K4, P3, K1, P7, K7.

Row 45: K9, P2, K1, P5, K3, P7, K8.

Row 47: K 11, P 11, K2, P2, K9.

Row 49: K 11, P 11, K 13.

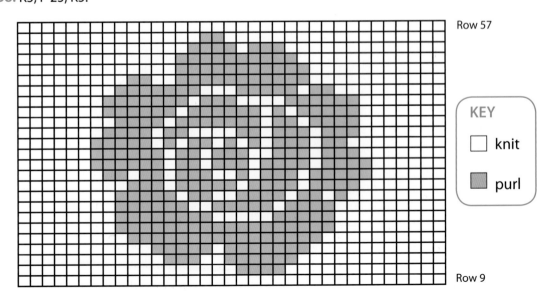

Row 57

Row 9

KEY

☐ knit

▨ purl

Row 51: K 12, P 10, K 13.

Row 53: K 13, P3, K1, P4, K 14.

Row 55: K 18, P2, K 15.

Row 57: Knit across.

Rows 59-65: Knit across.

Bind off all sts in **knit**.

Cast on 35 sts.

Rows 1-7: Knit across.

Row 8 AND ALL WRONG SIDE ROWS THROUGH Row 58: K5, P 25, K5.

Row 9: Knit across.

Row 11: K6, P5, K1, P1, K3, P1, K1, P5, K1, P1, K3, P1, K6.

Row 13: K 10, P1, K1, P2, K2, P1, (K3, P1) twice, (K1, P1) twice, K6.

Row 15: K8, P3, (K1, P1) 3 times, (K3, P1) twice, (K1, P1) twice, K6.

Row 17: K 10, P1, K1, P1, K2, P2, K3, P1, K3, P2, K1, P2, K6.

Row 19: K6, P5, K1, P1, K3, P1, K1, P5, K1, P1, K3, P1, K6.

Rows 21 and 23: Knit across.

Row 25: K 17, P1, K 17.

Row 27: K 16, P3, K 16.

Row 29: K 15, P5, K 15.

Row 31: K 14, P7, K 14.

Rows 33 and 35: K 13, P9, K 13.

Row 37: K 13, P4, K1, P4, K 13.

Row 39: K 14, P2, K3, P2, K 14.

Rows 41 and 43: Knit across.

Row 45: K 11, P5, K4, P4, K 11.

Row 47: K 15, P1, (K3, P1) twice, K 11.

Row 49: K 13, P3, K4, P4, K 11.

Row 51: K 15, P1, (K3, P1) twice, K 11.

Row 53: K 11, P5, K4, P4, K 11.

Rows 55 and 57: Knit across.

Rows 59-65: Knit across.

Bind off all sts in **knit**.

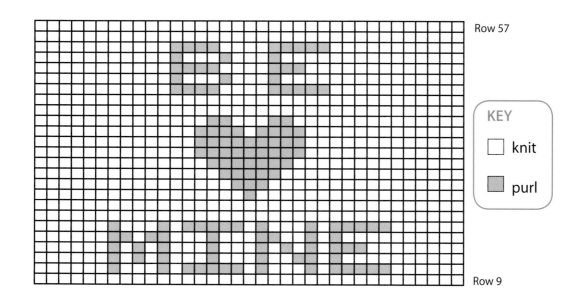

Row 57

KEY

☐ knit

▨ purl

Row 9

ST. PATRICK'S DAY

 **BEGINNER**

Finished Size:
7¾"w x 9¾"h (19.5 cm x 25 cm)

The **dishcloths** can be made by following the written instructions or by following the chart for Rows 9-57 *(see Charts, page 30)*. Only **odd numbered** rows are charted. Refer to Row 8 for all **even numbered** rows.

SHOPPING LIST

Yarn (Medium Weight Cotton)
[2.5 ounces, 120 yards  (71 grams, 109 meters) per ball]:
☐ One ball for **each** Dishcloth

Knitting Needles
☐ Straight, size 8 (5 mm)
or size needed for gauge

GAUGE INFORMATION

In Stockinette Stitch
(knit one row, purl one row),
9 sts and 13 rows = 2" (5 cm)

INSTRUCTIONS
Clover

Cast on 35 sts.

Rows 1-7: Knit across.

Row 8 AND ALL WRONG SIDE ROWS THROUGH Row 58: K5, P 25, K5.

Row 9: Knit across.

Row 11: K 14, P3, K 18.

Rows 13 and 15: K 15, P3, K 17.

Row 17: K 16, P2, K3, P2, K 12.

Row 19: K 11, P4, K1, P2, K2, P4, K 11.

Row 21: K 10, P8, K1, P7, K9.

Row 23: K 10, P8, K1, P8, K8.

Row 25: K9, P 19, K7.

Row 27: K8, P 20, K7.

Row 29: K7, P 20, K8.

Row 31: K7, P 19, K9.

Row 33: K7, P 18, K 10.

Row 35: K8, P 18, K9.

Row 37: K 11, P 17, K7.

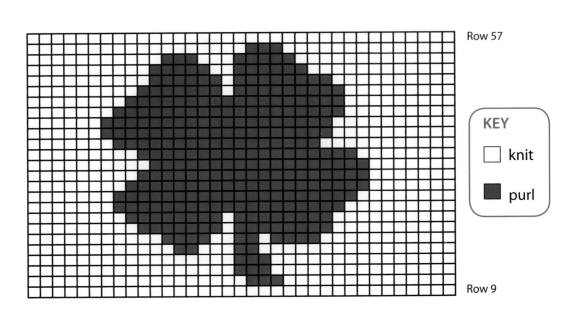

Row 57

Row 9

KEY
☐ knit
■ purl

Pot of Gold

Mug of Ale

Clover

Rows 39 and 41: K 10, P 19, K6.

Row 43: K9, P 19, K7.

Row 45: K9, P 18, K8.

Row 47: K9, P9, K1, P7, K9.

Row 49: K 10, P8, K1, P6, K 10.

Row 51: K 12, P6, K2, P5, K 10.

Row 53: K 13, P5, K3, P3, K 11.

Row 55: K 14, P3, K 18.

Row 57: Knit across.

Rows 59-65: Knit across.

Bind off all sts in **knit**.

Pot of Gold

Cast on 35 sts.

Rows 1-7: Knit across.

Row 8 AND ALL WRONG SIDE ROWS THROUGH Row 58: K5, P 25, K5.

Rows 9, 11, and 13: Knit across.

Row 15: K 10, P2, K5, P1, K5, P2, K 10.

Row 17: K9, P4, K3, P3, K3, P4, K9.

Rows 19 and 21: K 10, P 15, K 10.

Row 23: K8, P 19, K8.

Rows 25, 27, and 29: K7, P 21, K7.

Row 31: K8, P 19, K8.

Row 33: K9, P 17, K9.

Row 35: K8, P5, K9, P5, K8.

Row 37: K 10, P1, K3, P1, K1, P1, (K3, P1) twice, K 10.

Row 39: K8, P1, K2, P2, K5, P1, K3, P2, K2, P1, K8.

Row 41: K7, P1, K5, P1, K2, P1, K3, P2, K5, P1, K7.

Row 43: K6, (P1, K3) twice, P2, K1, P3, K3, P1, K4, P1, K6.

Row 45: K9, P1, K 14, P1, K 10.

Row 57

Row 9

KEY

□ knit

■ purl

Row 47: K8, P1, K4, P1, K6, P1, K4, P1, K9.

Row 49: K 12, P1, K8, P1, K 13.

Row 51: K 11, P1, K 10, P1, K 12.

Rows 53, 55, and 57: Knit across.

Rows 59-65: Knit across.

Bind off all sts in **knit**.

Mug of Ale

Cast on 35 sts.

Rows 1-7: Knit across.

Row 8 AND ALL WRONG SIDE ROWS THROUGH Row 58: K5, P 25, K5.

Rows 9, 11, and 13: Knit across.

Row 15: K 14, P8, K 13.

Rows 17, 19, and 21: K 13, P 10, K 12.

Row 23: K 11, P 12, K 12.

Row 25: K 10, P 13, K 12.

Row 27: K9, P3, K1, P 10, K 12.

Rows 29, 31, and 33: K9, P2, K2, P 10, K 12.

Row 35: K9, P3, K1, P 11, K 11.

Row 37: K 10, P 13, K1, P1, K 10.

Row 39: K 11, P 12, K1, P1, K 10.

Row 41: K 13, P3, K1, P2, K2, P1, K3, P1, K9. *Check - This is top of mug*

Row 43: (K 12, P1) twice, K9.

Row 45: K 12, P1, K 11, P1, K 10.

Row 47: K 12, P1, K 10, P1, K 11.

Row 49: K 13, P3, K5, P2, K 12.

Row 51: K 16, P5, K 14. *Check top of steam if coffee*

Rows 53, 55, and 57: Knit across.

Rows 59-65: Knit across.

Bind off all sts in **knit**.

Row 57

Row 9

KEY

☐ knit
■ purl

EASTER

Finished Size:

7¾"w x 9¾"h (19.5 cm x 25 cm)

The **dishcloths** can be made by following the written instructions or by following the chart for Rows 9-57 *(see Charts, page 30)*. Only **odd numbered** rows are charted. Refer to Row 8 for all **even numbered** rows.

SHOPPING LIST

Yarn (Medium Weight Cotton)
[2.5 ounces, 120 yards **MEDIUM 4**
(71 grams, 109 meters) per ball]:

☐ One ball for **each** Dishcloth

Knitting Needles

☐ Straight, size 8 (5 mm)

or size needed for gauge

GAUGE INFORMATION

In Stockinette Stitch
   (knit one row, purl one row),
   9 sts and 13 rows = 2" (5 cm)

INSTRUCTIONS
Bunny

Cast on 35 sts.

Rows 1-7: Knit across.

Row 8 AND ALL WRONG SIDE ROWS THROUGH Row 58: K5, P 25, K5.

Row 9: Knit across.

Row 11: K 13, P9, K 13.

Row 13: K 12, P4, K3, P4, K 12.

Rows 15 and 17: K 11, P4, K5, P4, K 11.

Row 19: K 11, P5, K3, P5, K 11.

Row 21: K 12, P 11, K 12.

Row 23: K 13, P9, K 13.

Rows 25 and 27: K 14, P7, K 14.

Row 29: K 15, P5, K 15.

Row 31: K 16, P3, K 16.

Row 33: K 15, P5, K 15.

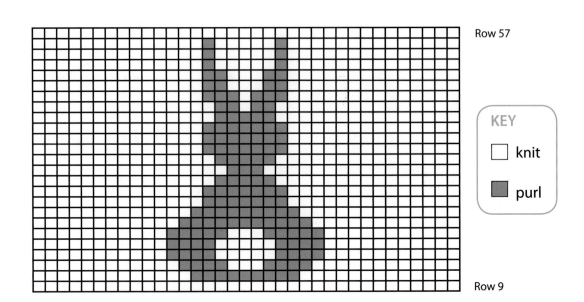

Row 57

Row 9

KEY

☐ knit

■ purl

Bunny

Egg

Cross

Rows 35, 37, and 39: K 14, P7, K 14.

Row 41: K 15, P5, K 15.

Row 43: K 15, P2, K1, P2, K 15.

Row 45: K 14, P3, K1, P3, K 14.

Rows 47 and 49: K 14, P2, K3, P2, K 14.

Rows 51, 53, and 55: K 14, P1, K5, P1, K 14.

Row 57: Knit across.

Rows 59-65: Knit across.

Bind off all sts in **knit**.

Cross

Cast on 35 sts.

Rows 1-7: Knit across.

Row 8 AND ALL WRONG SIDE ROWS THROUGH Row 58: K5, P 25, K5.

Rows 9 and 11: Knit across.

Rows 13, 15, 17, 19, 21, 23, 25, 27, 29, 31, and 33: K 15, P5, K 15.

Rows 35, 37, 39, 41, and 43: K 10, P 15, K 10.

Rows 45, 47, 49, 51, and 53: K 15, P5, K 15.

Rows 55 and 57: Knit across.

Rows 59-65: Knit across.

Bind off all sts in **knit**.

Egg

Cast on 35 sts.

Rows 1-7: Knit across.

Row 8 AND ALL WRONG SIDE ROWS THROUGH Row 58: K5, P 25, K5.

Row 9: Knit across.

Row 11: K 13, P9, K 13.

Row 13: K 11, P2, K3, P1, K5, P2, K 11.

Row 15: K 10, P1, K4, P1, K1, P1, K6, P1, K 10.

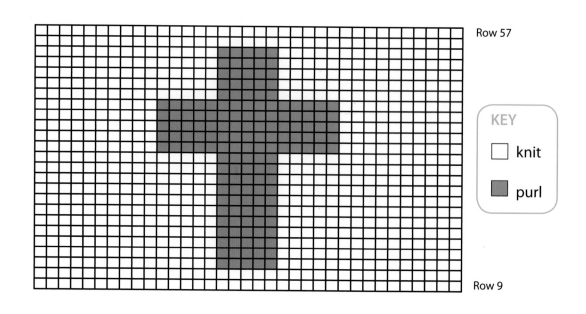

Row 57

Row 9

KEY

☐ knit

▨ purl

Row 17: K9, P1, K6, P1, K5, P1, K2, P1, K9.

Row 19: K9, P1, K 11, P1, (K1, P1) twice, K9.

Row 21: K8, P1, K4, P1, K8, P1, K3, P1, K8.

Row 23: K8, P1, K3, P1, K1, P1, K 11, P1, K8.

Row 25: K8, P1, (K4, P1) twice, K7, P1, K8.

Row 27: (K8, P1) twice, K1, P1, K6, P1, K8.

Row 29: K8, P1, K9, P1, K4, P1, K2, P1, K8.

Row 31: K8, P1, K1, P1, K 11, P1, (K1, P1) twice, K8.

Row 33: K8, P2, K1, P1, K 11, P1, K2, P1, K8.

Row 35: K8, P1, K1, P1, K5, P1, K9, P1, K8.

Row 37: K8, P1, K6, P1, K1, (P1, K8) twice.

Row 39: K8, P1, K7, P1, (K4, P1) twice, K8.

Row 41: K9, P1, K2, P1, K7, P1, K1, P1, K2, P1, K9.

Row 43: K9, P1, (K1, P1) twice, K7, P1, K3, P1, K9.

Row 45: K 10, P1, K1, P1, K 11, P1, K 10.

Row 47: K 10, P1, (K6, P1) twice, K 10.

Row 49: K 11, P1, K4, P1, K1, P1, K4, P1, K 11.

Row 51: K 12, P1, (K4, P1) twice, K 12.

Row 53: K 13, P2, K5, P2, K 13.

Row 55: K 15, P5, K 15.

Row 57: Knit across.

Rows 59-65: Knit across.

Bind off all sts in **knit**.

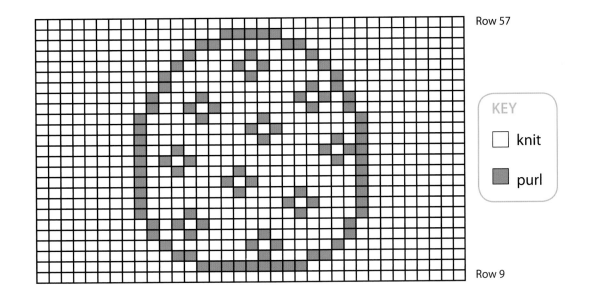

Row 57

Row 9

KEY

☐ knit

▨ purl

INDEPENDENCE DAY

 BEGINNER

Finished Size:

7¾"w x 9¾"h (19.5 cm x 25 cm)

The **dishcloths** can be made by following the written instructions or by following the chart for Rows 9-57 *(see Charts, page 30)*. Only **odd numbered** rows are charted. Refer to Row 8 for all **even numbered** rows.

SHOPPING LIST

Yarn (Medium Weight Cotton)

[2.5 ounces, 120 yards **MEDIUM 4** (71 grams, 109 meters) per ball]:

☐ One ball for **each** Dishcloth

Knitting Needles

☐ Straight, size 8 (5 mm)

or size needed for gauge

GAUGE INFORMATION

In Stockinette Stitch

(knit one row, purl one row),

9 sts and 13 rows = 2" (5 cm)

INSTRUCTIONS
Fireworks

Cast on 35 sts.

Rows 1-7: Knit across.

Row 8 AND ALL WRONG SIDE ROWS THROUGH Row 58: K5, P 25, K5.

Row 9: Knit across.

Rows 11 and 13: K 26, P1, K8.

Rows 15 and 17: K 25, P1, K9.

Row 19: K 18, P1, K5, P1, K 10.

Row 21: K 13, (P1, K 10) twice.

Row 23: K 18, P1, K4, P1, K 11.

Row 25: K 13, P1, K8, P1, K 12.

Row 27: K9, P1, K8, P1, K2, P1, K 13.

Row 29: K 14, P1, K5, P1, K 14.

Row 31: K9, P1, K6, P2, K 17.

Row 33: K 11, P1, K3, P1, K1, P2, K2, P1, (K1, P1) twice, K9.

Row 35: K 14, P3, K1, P2, K 15.

Row 37: K 13, P1, K1, P3, K1, P1, K 15.

Row 39: K9, P1, K2, P3, K1, P3, K 16.

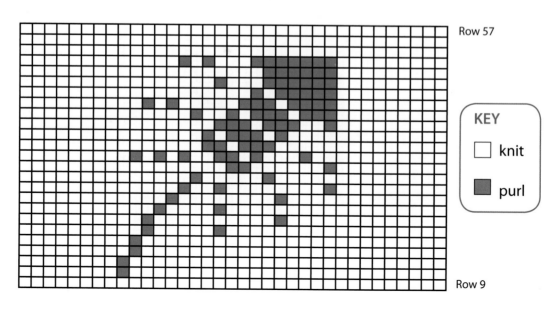

Row 57

Row 9

KEY

☐ knit

■ purl

4th of July

Uncle Sam's Hat

Fireworks

Row 41: K9, (P3, K1) twice, P1, K2, P1, K 14.

Row 43: K9, P4, K1, P3, K5, P1, K1, P1, K 10.

Row 45: K9, P5, K1, P1, K 19.

Row 47: K9, P6, K3, P1, K 16.

Row 49: K9, P6, K 20.

Row 51: K9, P7, K3, P1, K1, P1, K 13.

Rows 53, 55, and 57: Knit across.

Rows 59-65: Knit across.

Bind off all sts in **knit**.

4th of July

Cast on 35 sts.

Rows 1-7: Knit across.

Row 8 AND ALL WRONG SIDE ROWS THROUGH Row 58: K5, P 25, K5.

Row 9: Knit across.

Row 11: K8, P2, K2, P5, K2, P3, K3, P3, K7.

Row 13: K8, P2, K2, P5, (K1, P5) twice, K6.

Row 15: K8, P2, K2, P2, (K1, P2) 5 times, K6.

Row 17: K7, P4, K4, P2, (K1, P2) 3 times, K9.

Row 19: K6, P6, K3, P2, (K1, P2) 3 times, K9.

Rows 21, 23, and 25: K6, P2, K2, P2, K3, P2, (K1, P2) 3 times, K9.

Row 27: Knit across.

Rows 29 and 31: K 13, P2, K3, P5, K 12.

Row 33: K 12, P4, K2, P2, K1, P2, K 12.

Row 35: K 12, P4, K2, P5, K 12.

Row 37: K 13, P2, K3, P5, K 12.

Rows 39 and 41: K 11, P4, K 20.

Row 43: K 21, P2, K 12.

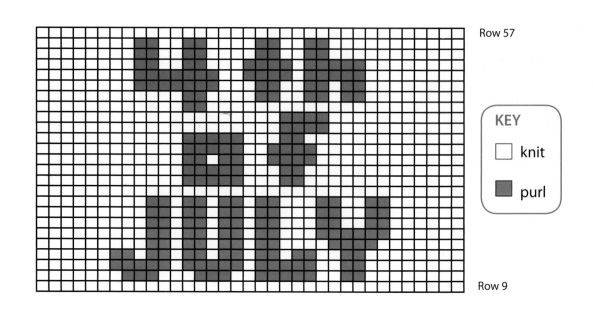

Row 57

Row 9

KEY

☐ knit

■ purl

Row 45: K8, P2, K1, P2, K2, P2, K4, P2, K 12.

Row 47: K8, P2, K1, P2, K2, P2, K3, P7, K8.

Row 49: K8, P5, K1, P4, K2, P7, K8.

Row 51: K8, P5, K1, P4, K3, P2, K2, P2, K8.

Rows 53 and 55: K 11, P2, K2, P2, K4, P2, K2, P2, K8.

Row 57: Knit across.

Rows 59-65: Knit across.

Bind off all sts in **knit**.

Uncle Sam's Hat

Cast on 35 sts.

Rows 1-7: Knit across.

Row 8 AND ALL WRONG SIDE ROWS THROUGH Row 58: K5, P 25, K5.

Rows 9 and 11: Knit across.

Row 13: K7, P 21, K7.

Rows 15 and 17: K6, P1, K 21, P1, K6.

Row 19: K7, P 21, K7.

Row 21: K 10, P2, K1, P1, K1, P5, K1, P1, K1, P2, K 10.

Row 23: K 10, P2, K3, P5, K3, P2, K 10.

Row 25: K 10, P1, K5, P3, K5, P1, K 10.

Row 27: K 10, P3, K1, P7, K1, P3, K 10.

Row 29: K 10, P 15, K 10.

Rows 31, 33, 35, 37, 39, 41, 43, 45, 47, 49, and 51: K 10, P3, (K3, P3) twice, K 10.

Row 53: K 10, P 15, K 10.

Rows 55 and 57: Knit across.

Rows 59-65: Knit across.

Bind off all sts in **knit**.

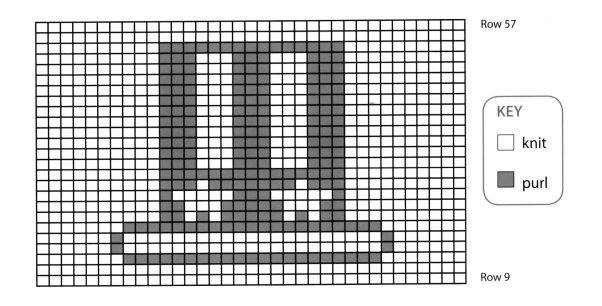

Row 57

Row 9

KEY

☐ knit

▨ purl

17

HALLOWEEN

Finished Size:

7¾"w x 9¾"h (19.5 cm x 25 cm)

SHOPPING LIST

Yarn (Medium Weight Cotton)
[2.5 ounces, 120 yards **MEDIUM 4**
(71 grams, 109 meters) per ball]:

☐ One ball for **each** Dishcloth

Knitting Needles

☐ Straight, size 8 (5 mm)
  or size needed for gauge

GAUGE INFORMATION

In Stockinette Stitch
  (knit one row, purl one row),
  9 sts and 13 rows = 2" (5 cm)

The **dishcloths** can be made by following the written instructions or by following the chart for Rows 9-57 *(see Charts, page 30)*. Only **odd numbered** rows are charted. Refer to Row 8 for all **even numbered** rows.

INSTRUCTIONS
Pumpkin

Cast on 35 sts.

Rows 1-7: Knit across.

Row 8 AND ALL WRONG SIDE ROWS THROUGH Row 58: K5, P 25, K5.

Row 9: Knit across.

Row 11: K 13, P9, K 13.

Row 13: K 11, P 13, K 11.

Row 15: K9, P 17, K9.

Row 17: K8, P5, K9, P5, K8.

Row 19: K7, P4, K 13, P4, K7.

Row 21: K6, P4, K5, P1, K3, P1, K5, P4, K6.

Row 23: K6, P3, K3, P 11, K3, P3, K6.

Row 25: K6, P2, K2, P 15, K2, P2, K6.

Row 27: K6, P2, K1, P5, K7, P5, K1, P2, K6.

Row 29: K6, P9, K5, P9, K6.

Row 31: K6, P 10, K3, P 10, K6.

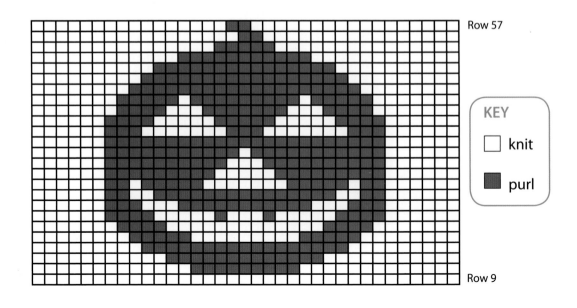

Row 57

Row 9

KEY

☐ knit

■ purl

Bat

Cat

Pumpkin

Row 33: K6, P 11, K1, P 11, K6.

Row 35: K6, P 23, K6.

Row 37: K6, P3, (K7, P3) twice, K6.

Row 39: K6, P4, K5, P5, K5, P4, K6.

Row 41: K7, P4, K3, P7, K3, P4, K7.

Row 43: K7, P5, K1, P9, K1, P5, K7.

Row 45: K8, P 19, K8.

Row 47: K9, P 17, K9.

Row 49: K 10, P 15, K 10.

Row 51: K 12, P 11, K 12.

Row 53: K 15, P5, K 15.

Row 55: K 16, P2, K 17.

Row 57: K 17, P2, K 16.

Rows 59-65: Knit across.

Bind off all sts in **knit**.

Bat

Cast on 35 sts.

Rows 1-7: Knit across.

Row 8 AND ALL WRONG SIDE ROWS THROUGH Row 58: K5, P 25, K5.

Row 9: Knit across.

Row 11: K 28, P1, K6.

Row 13: K 27, P2, K6.

Rows 15 and 17: K 26, P3, K6.

Rows 19 and 21: K 22, P7, K6.

Row 23: K 12, P6, K3, P8, K6.

Rows 25, 27, 29, and 31: K 12, P 17, K6.

Row 33: K 12, P 12, K 11.

Row 35: K 13, P 11, K 11.

Rows 37 and 39: K 13, P 10, K 12.

Row 41: K 12, P 13, K 10.

Row 43: K 10, P 15, K 10.

Row 45: K 10, P9, K2, P3, K1, P1, K9.

Row 47: K 10, P7, K4, P2, K 12.

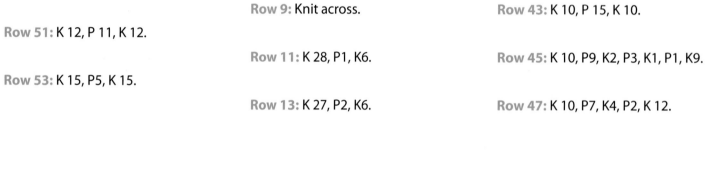

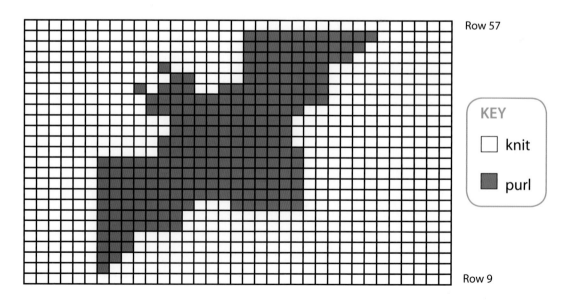

Row 57

Row 9

KEY

☐ knit

■ purl

Row 49: K 10, P7, K6, P1, K 11.

Row 51: K8, P9, K 18.

Row 53: K7, P 10, K 18.

Row 55: K6, P 11, K 18.

Row 57: Knit across.

Rows 59-65: Knit across.

Bind off all sts in **knit**.

Cat

Cast on 35 sts.

Rows 1-7: Knit across.

Row 8 AND ALL WRONG SIDE ROWS
THROUGH Row 58: K5, P 25, K5.

Row 9: Knit across.

Row 11: K 11, P2, K1, P2, K7, P2, K 10.

Row 13: K 12, P1, K2, P1, K8, P2, K9.

Row 15: K 12, P2, K1, P2, K8, P1, K9.

Row 17: K 12, P2, K1, P2, K7, P2, K9.

Row 19: K 12, P2, K1, P2, K6, P3, K9.

Rows 21 and 23: K 13, P4, K5, P3, K 10.

Row 25: K9, P8, K5, P4, K9.

Row 27: K8, P 11, K2, P5, K9.

Row 29: K8, P 19, K8.

Row 31: K9, P 18, K8.

Row 33: K 10, P3, K1, P 14, K7.

Row 35: K 10, P1, K4, P 13, K7.

Row 37: K 15, P 10, K1, P2, K7.

Row 39: K 16, P9, K1, P2, K7.

Row 41: K 17, P7, K2, P2, K7.

Row 43: K 19, P4, K4, P1, K7.

Rows 45, 47, 49, 51, and 53: K 27, P1, K7.

Rows 55 and 57: Knit across.

Rows 59-65: Knit across.

Bind off all sts in **knit**.

Row 57

Row 9

KEY

☐ knit

▨ purl

21

THANKSGIVING

 **BEGINNER**

Finished Size:

7¾"w x 9¾"h (19.5 cm x 25 cm)

SHOPPING LIST

Yarn (Medium Weight Cotton)

[2.5 ounces, 120 yards **MEDIUM 4**

(71 grams, 109 meters) per ball]:

☐ One ball for **each** Dishcloth

Knitting Needles

☐ Straight, size 8 (5 mm)

or size needed for gauge

GAUGE INFORMATION

In Stockinette Stitch

(knit one row, purl one row),

9 sts and 13 rows = 2" (5 cm)

The **dishcloths** can be made by following the written instructions or by following the chart for Rows 9-57 (see Charts, page 30). Only **odd numbered** rows are charted. Refer to Row 8 for all **even numbered** rows.

INSTRUCTIONS
Praying Hands

Cast on 35 sts.

Rows 1-7: Knit across.

Row 8 AND ALL WRONG SIDE ROWS THROUGH Row 58: K5, P 25, K5.

Rows 9 and 11: Knit across.

Row 13: K7, P 16, K2, P2, K8.

Row 15: K7, P 15, K2, P3, K8.

Row 17: K7, P 10, K2, P2, K2, P3, K9.

Row 19: K7, P9, K2, P2, K2, P4, K9.

Row 21: K7, P8, K1, P1, K3, P2, K1, P2, K 10.

Row 23: K8, P7, K1, P4, K2, P1, K 12.

Row 25: K9, P5, K1, P7, K1, P1, K 11.

Row 27: K 10, P4, K1, P2, K1, P5, K1, P1, K 10.

Row 29: K 11, P2, K1, P1, K2, P7, K1, P1, K9.

Row 31: K 13, P1, K1, P9, K1, P1, K9.

Rows 33 and 35: K 15, P 10, K1, P1, K8.

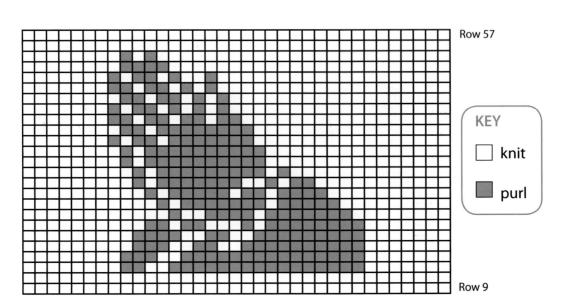

Row 57

Row 9

KEY

☐ knit

■ purl

Turkey

Corn

Praying Hands

Row 37: K 16, P7, K1, P2, K1, P1, K7.

Row 39: K 16, P8, K1, P2, K8.

Row 41: K 17, P2, (K1, P2) 3 times, K7.

Row 43: K 18, (P1, K1) 3 times, P2, K1, P1, K7.

Row 45: K 18, (P1, K1) twice, P2, K1, P2, K8.

Row 47: K 19, (P1, K1) twice, P2, K1, P2, K7.

Row 49: K 19, P1, K2, P1, K1, P2, K1, P1, K7.

Row 51: K 23, P4, K8.

Row 53: K 24, P1, K1, P1, K8.

Rows 55 and 57: Knit across.

Rows 59-65: Knit across.

Bind off all sts in **knit**.

Row 11: K 13, P3, K3, P3, K 13.

Row 13: K 15, P5, K 15.

Row 15: K 14, P7, K 14.

Row 17: K 11, P 13, K 11.

Row 19: K 10, P1, K1, P2, K1, P5, K1, P2, K1, P1, K 10.

Row 21: K9, P1, K2, P3, (K1, P3) twice, K2, P1, K9.

Row 23: K8, P1, K3, P3, (K1, P3) twice, K3, P1, K8.

Row 25: K7, P1, K3, P 13, K3, P1, K7.

Row 27: K6, P1, K3, P1, K2, P9, K2, P1, K3, P1, K6.

Row 29: K6, P1, K2, P1, K4, P7, K4, P1, K2, P1, K6.

Row 31: K6, P3, K4, P1, K1, P5, K1, P1, K4, P3, K6.

Row 33: K7, P1, K4, P1, K3, P1, K1, P1, K3, P1, K4, P1, K7.

Row 35: K6, P1, K4, P1, K3, P2, K1, P2, K3, P1, K4, P1, K6.

Row 37: K6, P1, K3, P1, K4, P5, K4, P1, K3, P1, K6.

Row 39: K7, P3, K4, P2, K1, P1, K1, P2, K4, P3, K7.

Row 41: K9, P1, K3, P1, K1, P5, K1, P1, K3, P1, K9.

Row 43: K9, P1, K2, P1, K3, P3, K3, P1, K2, P1, K9.

Row 45: K 10, P2, K4, P1, K1, P1, K4, P2, K 10.

Row 47: K 12, P1, K2, P1, K3, P1, K2, P1, K 12.

Row 49: K 13, P3, K3, P3, K 13.

Row 51: K 16, P1, K1, P1, K 16.

Turkey

Cast on 35 sts.

Rows 1-7: Knit across.

Row 8 AND ALL WRONG SIDE ROWS THROUGH Row 58: K5, P 25, K5.

Row 9: Knit across.

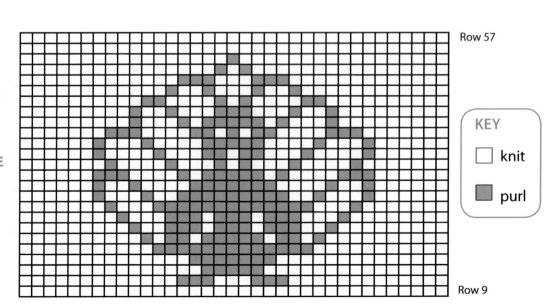

Row 57

Row 9

KEY

☐ knit

▨ purl

Row 53: K 17, P1, K 17.

Rows 55 and 57: Knit across.

Rows 59-65: Knit across.

Bind off all sts in **knit**.

Corn

Cast on 35 sts.

Rows 1-7: Knit across.

Row 8 AND ALL WRONG SIDE ROWS THROUGH Row 58: K5, P 25, K5.

Row 9: Knit across.

Row 11: K 22, P4, K9.

Row 13: K 20, P2, K2, P3, K8.

Row 15: K 17, P3, K3, P1, (K1, P1) twice, K7.

Row 17: K 14, P3, K4, P2, K2, P1, K1, P1, K7.

Row 19: K9, P5, K6, P1, K2, P2, K2, P1, K7.

Row 21: K8, P2, K9, P1, K2, P1, K1, P1, K3, P1, K6.

Row 23: K7, P6, K4, P2, K3, P1, K1, P1, K3, P1, K6.

Row 25: K9, P2, K2, P4, K4, P1, K2, P1, K3, P1, K6.

Row 27: K 10, P3, K6, P3, K1, P1, K4, P1, K6.

Row 29: K 10, P1, K2, P6, K1, P1, K2, P1, K4, P1, K6.

Row 31: K9, P1, K2, P2, K1, (P1, K1) twice, P2, K2, P1, K4, P1, K6.

Row 33: K8, P1, K2, P2, (K1, P1) 4 times, K2, P1, K4, P1, K6.

Row 35: K7, P5, K1, (P1, K1) 3 times, P2, K2, P1, K3, P1, K7.

Row 37: K9, P2, (K1, P1) 5 times, K2, P1, K3, P1, K7.

Row 39: K8, P2, K1, (P1, K1) 4 times, P3, (K2, P1) twice, K7.

Row 41: K8, (P1, K1) 5 times, P2, K1, P1, K2, P1, K1, P1, K8.

Row 43: K7, (P1, K1) 5 times, P2, K2, P2, (K1, P1) twice, K8.

Row 45: K7, P2, K1, (P1, K1) 3 times, P2, K3, P2, K1, P2, K9.

Row 47: K7, (P1, K1) 4 times, P3, K2, (P1, K1) twice, P2, K9.

Row 49: K7, P2, K1, (P1, K1) twice, P2, K1, (P1, K2) twice, P3, K9.

Row 51: K7, (P1, K1) 3 times, P2, K2, P1, K1, P1, K4, P3, K8.

Row 53: K7, P6, K5, P1, K 16.

Row 55: K 18, P1, K 16.

Row 57: Knit across.

Rows 59-65: Knit across.

Bind off all sts in **knit**.

Row 57

Row 9

KEY

☐ knit

▧ purl

CHRISTMAS

Finished Size:

7¾"w x 9¾"h (19.5 cm x 25 cm)

The **dishcloths** can be made by following the written instructions or by following the chart for Rows 9-57 *(see Charts, page 30)*. Only **odd numbered** rows are charted. Refer to Row 8 for all **even numbered** rows.

SHOPPING LIST

Yarn (Medium Weight Cotton)
[2.5 ounces, 120 yards **MEDIUM 4**
(71 grams, 109 meters) per ball]:

☐ One ball for **each** Dishcloth

Knitting Needles

☐ Straight, size 8 (5 mm)

 or size needed for gauge

GAUGE INFORMATION

In Stockinette Stitch

 (knit one row, purl one row),

 9 sts and 13 rows = 2" (5 cm)

INSTRUCTIONS
Stocking

Cast on 35 sts.

Rows 1-7: Knit across.

Row 8 AND ALL WRONG SIDE ROWS THROUGH Row 58: K5, P 25, K5.

Row 9: K 18, P5, K 12.

Row 11: K 17, P1, K5, P1, K 11.

Row 13: K 16, P2, K6, P1, K 10.

Row 15: K 15, P4, K6, P1, K9.

Row 17: K 14, P5, K6, P1, K9.

Row 19: K 11, P9, K5, P1, K9.

Row 21: K9, P 13, K3, P1, K9.

Row 23: K8, P1, K2, P 14, K 10.

Row 25: K7, P1, K4, P 12, K 11.

Row 27: K7, P1, K4, P 11, K 12.

Row 29: K7, P1, K4, P 10, K 13.

Rows 31 and 33: K8, P1, K2, P 10, K 14.

Row 35: K9, P 13, K 13.

Row 57

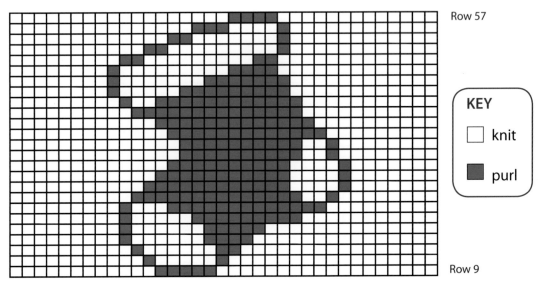

Row 9

KEY

☐ knit

■ purl

Christmas Tree

Stocking

Candy Cane

Row 37: K 10, P 13, K 12.

Row 39: K 11, P 14, K 10.

Row 41: K 11, P 12, K2, P1, K9.

Row 43: K 12, P9, K5, P1, K8.

Row 45: K 12, P7, K7, P1, K8.

Row 47: K 13, P4, K9, P1, K8.

Row 49: K 13, (P2, K9) twice.

Row 51: K 12, P1, K9, P2, K 11.

Row 53: K 12, P1, K7, P2, K 13.

Row 55: K 12, P1, K4, P3, K 15.

Row 57: K 13, P4, K 18.

Rows 59-65: Knit across.

Bind off all sts in **knit**.

Cast on 35 sts.

Rows 1-7: Knit across.

Row 8 AND ALL WRONG SIDE ROWS THROUGH Row 58: K5, P 25, K5.

Row 9: Knit across.

Row 11: K 19, P3, K 13.

Row 13: K 18, P1, K2, P2, K 12.

Row 15: K 18, P1, K3, P1, K 12.

Row 17: K 18, P2, K2, P1, K 12.

Row 19: K 18, P3, K1, P1, K 12.

Rows 21, 23, and 25: K 18, P5, K 12.

Row 27: K 18, P1, K1, P3, K 12.

Row 29: K 18, P1, K2, P2, K 12.

Row 31: K 18, P1, K3, P1, K 12.

Row 33: K 11, P3, K4, P2, K2, P1, K 12.

Row 35: K 10, P5, K3, P3, K1, P1, K 12.

Row 37: K 10, P5, K3, P5, K 12.

Row 39: K 10, P3, K1, P1, K3, P5, K 12.

Row 41: K 10, P2, K2, P1, K3, P5, K 12.

Row 43: K 10, P1, (K3, P1) twice, K1, P3, K 12.

Row 45: K 10, P1, K2, P5, K3, P2, K 12.

Row 47: K 10, P1, K1, P7, K3, P1, K 12.

Row 49: K 10, P6, K1, P3, K1, P1, K 13.

Row 51: K 11, P4, K2, P5, K 13.

Row 53: K 12, P2, K3, P4, K 14.

Row 55: K 13, P7, K 15.

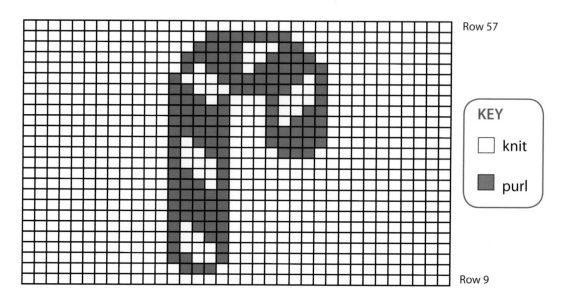

Row 57

Row 9

KEY

☐ knit

■ purl

Row 57: Knit across.

Rows 59-65: Knit across.

Bind off all sts in **knit**.

Christmas Tree

Cast on 35 sts.

Rows 1-7: Knit across.

Row 8 AND ALL WRONG SIDE ROWS THROUGH Row 58: K5, P 25, K5.

Row 9: Knit across.

Row 11: K 14, P7, K 14.

Row 13: K 15, P5, K 15.

Row 15: K 16, P3, K 16.

Row 17: K6, P 23, K6.

Row 19: K7, (P4, K1) twice, P3, K1, P5, K1, P1, K7.

Row 21: K8, P6, K1, P7, K1, P4, K8.

Row 23: K9, P2, K1, P6, K1, P5, K1, P1, K9.

Row 25: K8, P1, (K1, P5) 3 times, K8.

Row 27: K9, P4, K1, P5, K1, P3, K1, P2, K9.

Row 29: K 10, P7, K1, P7, K 10.

Row 31: K 11, P2, K1, P8, K1, P1, K 11.

Row 33: K 10, P5, K1, P3, K1, P5, K 10.

Row 35: K 11, P1, K1, P8, K1, P2, K 11.

Row 37: K 12, P4, K1, P6, K 12.

Row 39: K 13, P1, K1, P4, K1, P2, K 13.

Row 41: K 12, P5, K1, P3, K1, P1, K 12.

Row 43: K 13, P2, K1, P6, K 13.

Row 45: K 14, P4, K1, P2, K 14.

Row 47: K 15, P5, K 15.

Row 49: K 14, (P2, K1) twice, P1, K 14.

Row 51: K 15, P5, K 15.

Row 53: K 16, P1, K1, P1, K 16.

Row 55: K 17, P1, K 17.

Row 57: Knit across.

Rows 59-65: Knit across.

Bind off all sts in **knit**.

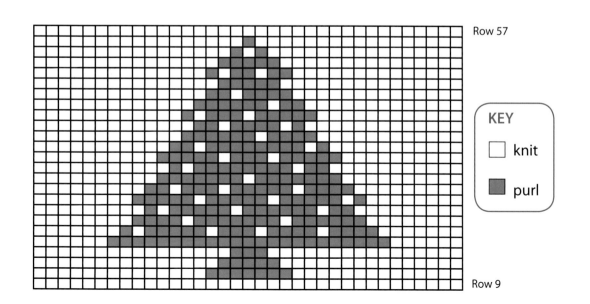

Row 57

Row 9

KEY

☐ knit

■ purl

GENERAL INSTRUCTIONS

ABBREVIATIONS

ch	chain
cm	centimeters
K	knit
mm	millimeters
P	purl
st(s)	stitch(es)

SYMBOLS & TERMS

( ) or [ ] — work enclosed instructions **as many** times as indicated by the number immediately following **or** contains explanatory remarks.

colon (:) — the number given after a colon at the end of a row denotes the number of stitches on that row.

GAUGE

The gauge and finished size given are for your convenience and are meant only as a guide. Gauge is not of great importance; your dishcloth can certainly be a little larger or smaller, without changing the overall effect.

CHARTS

You might find following a chart easier than following written instructions, as you can see what the pattern looks like and you can also see each row at a glance. If you've never knitted from a chart before, you can refer to the chart while you read the written instructions until you are comfortable with the process.

Visualize the chart as your fabric, beginning at the bottom edge and looking at the right side. The chart shows each stitch as a square.

Only **right** side rows are charted; follow the chart from **right** to **left**. Knit the white squares and purl the shaded squares.

For ease in following the chart, place a ruler on the chart above the row being worked to help you keep your place.

KNIT TERMINOLOGY	
UNITED STATES	**INTERNATIONAL**
gauge =	tension
bind off =	cast off
yarn over (YO) =	yarn forward (yfwd) **or** yarn around needle (yrn)

For complete instructions on knit basics and video support, visit www.leisurearts.com.

KNITTING NEEDLES																
U.S.	0	1	2	3	4	5	6	7	8	9	10	10½	11	13	15	17
U.K.	13	12	11	10	9	8	7	6	5	4	3	2	1	00	000	---
Metric - mm	2	2.25	2.75	3.25	3.5	3.75	4	4.5	5	5.5	6	6.5	8	9	10	12.75

■□□□ **BEGINNER**	Projects for first-time knitters using basic knit and purl stitches. Minimal shaping.
■■□□ **EASY**	Projects using basic stitches, repetitive stitch patterns, simple color changes, and simple shaping and finishing.
■■■□ **INTERMEDIATE**	Projects with a variety of stitches, such as basic cables and lace, simple intarsia, double-pointed needles and knitting in the round needle techniques, mid-level shaping and finishing.
■■■■ **EXPERIENCED**	Projects using advanced techniques and stitches, such as short rows, fair isle, more intricate intarsia, cables, lace patterns, and numerous color changes.

YARN INFORMATION

Each Dishcloth in this book was made using Medium Weight Cotton yarn. Any brand of Medium Weight Cotton yarn may be used. It is best to refer to the yardage/meters when determining how many balls or skeins to purchase. Remember, to arrive at the finished size, it is the GAUGE/TENSION that is important, not the brand of yarn. For your convenience, listed below are the specific yarns used to create our photography models.

VALENTINE'S DAY
Lily® Sugar 'n Cream®

Love - #01444 Mod Pink

Rose - #00095 Red

Be Mine - #00001 White

EASTER
Lily® Sugar 'n Cream®

Bunny - #00010 Yellow

Cross - #01712 Hot Green

Egg - #01444 Mod Pink

THANKSGIVING
Lily® Sugar 'n Cream®

Praying Hands - #00004 Ecru

Turkey - #01699 Tangerine

Corn - #01612 Country Yellow

ST. PATRICK'S DAY
Lily® Sugar 'n Cream®

Clover - #00016 Dk Pine

Pot of Gold - #01612 Country Yellow

Mug of Ale - #01223 Mod Green

INDEPENDENCE DAY
Lily® Sugar 'n Cream®

Fireworks - #01116 Blue Jeans

4th of July - #00001 White

Uncle Sam's Hat - #00095 Red

CHRISTMAS
Lily® Sugar 'n Cream®

Stocking - #00095 Red

Candy Cane - #00001 White

Christmas Tree - #00016 Dk Pine

HALLOWEEN
Lily® Sugar 'n Cream®

Pumpkin - #01628 Hot Orange

Bat - #01712 Hot Green

Cat - #00071 Grape

Yarn Weight Symbol & Names	LACE 0	SUPER FINE 1	FINE 2	LIGHT 3	MEDIUM 4	BULKY 5	SUPER BULKY 6
Type of Yarns in Category	Fingering, size 10 crochet thread	Sock, Fingering, Baby	Sport, Baby	DK, Light Worsted	Worsted, Afghan, Aran	Chunky, Craft, Rug	Bulky, Roving
Knit Gauge Range* in Stockinette St to 4" (10 cm)	33-40** sts	27-32 sts	23-26 sts	21-24 sts	16-20 sts	12-15 sts	6-11 sts
Advised Needle Size Range	000-1	1 to 3	3 to 5	5 to 7	7 to 9	9 to 11	11 and larger

*GUIDELINES ONLY: The chart above reflects the most commonly used gauges and needle sizes for specific yarn categories.

** Lace weight yarns are usually knitted on larger needles to create lacy openwork patterns. Accordingly, a gauge range is difficult to determine. Always follow the gauge stated in your pattern.

Meet Julie A. Ray

"I really enjoy the quickness of making dishcloths," says Julie Ray. "I encourage everyone to give knitting dishcloths a try — they're beginner-friendly, and they open a door to all kinds of projects. The possibilities are endless, and so is the joy of creating something for someone you love."

Julie says her creativity comes from her late mother, Shirley Smith. "She encouraged me in all that I did, including designing my own patterns." Julie not only knits, but she also crochets, sews, quilts, and does cross stitch, fitting lots of creativity into her busy days.

"My wonderful husband, Richard, is a chef," she says. "I have three children, two stepchildren, a daughter-in-law, and three grandkids, and I enjoy visiting with my dad, Darrel Smith."

Production Team: Instructional/Technical Writer - Linda A. Daley; Editorial Writer - Susan Frantz Wiles; Senior Graphic Artist - Lora Puls; Graphic Artist - Becca Snider Tally; Photo Stylist - Sondra Daniel; and Photographer - Ken West.

Instructions tested and photography models made by Margaret Taverner.